Self-Care with Sarah Reddan

Starting Your Self-Care Journey

Creating space to nourish you

To those who encourage me to stand in the light and share what I have to say, I thank you.

Copyright © Sarah Reddan 2022
ISBN: 9798832511313

Sarah Reddan has asserted her right under the Copyright, Designs and Patents Act 1988 to be identified as the author of this work.

All rights reserved. No portion of this book may be reproduced, copied, distributed, or adapted in any way, without the author's consent.

This book is intended for readers 18+

It is not intended to be a substitute for professional medical advice and should not be relied on as individual health or personal advice.

Table Of Contents:

Welcome to your self-care journey	7
Starting a self-care journey	12
Why self-care?	15
Who is Sarah Reddan?	18
What is self-care?	28
Barriers to self-care	33
Too busy	34
Fear	38
Feeling Overwhelmed	42
Conditioning messages	47
Time	50
Guilt	55
Not knowing what to do	57
Self-care is an act of love	60
How do you talk to yourself?	65
Self-Care Practice Activities	80
The power of meditation	93
What's next?	99

Welcome to your self-care journey

Self-care has become a word we use to describe having baths and facemasks or drinking a glass of wine after a hard day at work, a word we use but don't necessarily have a real understanding of, or a connection to…self-care may feel like a concept that other people do but that hasn't found a space within your life ……

YET……..

However, since you have picked up this book clearly you are yearning for something more and are ready to take the first steps on your journey to self-care.

This book has been created to gently guide you to start your self-care journey, through understanding why self-care is important for you, to gently challenge some of the thinking that may have been holding you back and to support you in creating space to build the foundations of your self-care practice.

You will gain information, suggestions, and inspiration, and be offered reflection questions and activities to help you connect to the path you want to take to create a self-care practice that works for you and your life.

This is the start of your journey of discovery, and I hope to encourage you to open your mind to fun, to be curious and kind to yourself, and to feel able to start to take action.

I hope reading this book supports you to create a life you love and that fills you up, that you connect with yourself and can relate to others in your life from a place of love and connection rather than exhaustion, frustration, and obligation.

This is your book and your self-care journey, so **you get to choose** how you wish to navigate it. You may wish to read this book all the way through from cover to cover or perhaps you would rather dip into the section that speaks to you the most right now.

We all KNOW that self-care is important but it's easy to feel that there isn't enough time or space in the busyness of day-to-day life to fit self-care tasks into our regular routine.

Self-care practices support not only your physical health but also your mental health, and emotional & spiritual needs.

I feel that TRUE self-care is the foundation for living an aligned life and that we are all here in this world to live a life that feels loving, kind, joyful and supported, and that those ways of being start with us and how we treat ourselves.

I WAS that person who put everyone else's needs above my own, who stayed in spaces & relationships that were not healthy for me, ignored my inner voice, and forgot how to have fun and this eventually led to me burning out.

I know that it can sometimes feel like change is impossible, that there is a massive gap from where you are now, in this moment, and to where you want to be, BUT taking small conscious, consistent steps really does help create the life you want.

The more you make space in your life to listen to your own needs and honour them the more you will generally find that this creates more happiness, more energy and space for deeper connections with those in your life.

There isn't a wrong way. However you choose to start your self-care journey is the right way for you!

This isn't a sprint, or a marathon – this is an exploration of new terrain, you are creating your own path and you can go at whatever pace supports you, allowing yourself the opportunity to create new habits, give yourself space to be curious and permission to play with creating what works for you.

Starting a self–care journey

Every person on a self-care journey will start at a different place, and the most important thing to remember as you go through this experience is that this is YOUR journey and the road that you take will most probably look different to those around you.

It may be that you already have habits that support you in your self-care, that you do without thinking about them, and haven't considered them as self-care before.

Perhaps you are at a stage where you have realised that you do very little for yourself and are ready to start to create habits that will help you.

Starting your self-care journey means that you will be bringing more attention to your own needs and are ready to start to create a life that fills you up first!

If you have been managing depression, stress, anxiety, or overwhelm, then daily tasks can at times feel difficult to achieve and if you are at a stage where daily washing, teeth brushing and a regular skincare routine sounds like hard work then things like regular massages, daily body movements, preparing nutritious meals, meditation and doing deep inner work may seem like a faraway dream. BUT we are going to start right at the very beginning, exactly where you are right now and create a mindset that supports you to create space and energy for daily self-care tasks to become manageable habits.

This book is about starting wherever you are now and taking teeny tiny steps towards that big picture of what self-care is for you.

As you read through this book you are going to be offered the opportunity to complete reflection tasks to support you, where there are questions, there is also space to record your thoughts in the book if you wish.

As you write, you are invited to be kind to yourself and focus on being open to creating the foundations of self-care, so you can start to create self-care practices that work for you.

Why self-care?

So many people, women especially, sacrifice who they are for the good of everyone around them and I genuinely believe that TRUE self-care, and by TRUE self-care I mean choosing to look after yourself first, is key to being fully present in your life & connected to those you choose to share it with.

True self-care is created by having boundaries, speaking your truth, knowing your own joy, knowing what ignites your soul and taking action to fill you up. True self-care allows you to ripple that care to those around you, so you come from a place of love and gratitude and giving because you want to, rather than from a place of guilt, resentment & anger.

True self-care is the underpinning factor of living your life the best way for you, living your life to the fullest and loving who you are. True self-care allows you to be you, all of you, in every place that you are.

Self-care means being loving and accepting towards yourself and showing yourself kindness and compassion.

Self-care means choosing a joyful life.

Self-care means modelling to your children (if you have them) how to love yourself.

Self-care means communicating your needs and your boundaries.

Self-care means allowing yourself time for you.

Self-care means trusting yourself.

Self-care means taking small steps & making small moments to honour yourself.

Self-care means you really do choose YOU and to allow yourself to live a life you love!

Because,

You are enough.

You are worthy.

And I want you to be able to know this in the core of who you are and the way in which you live your life moving forward.

Who is Sarah Reddan?

WHO AM I? This is a big question to answer about ourselves, isn't it?

Who Am I?

It's a question that is not always easy to answer for many of us, there are times I stumble over what my answer is, and some days the answer feels different.

So, let me start by sharing who I have been, and part of my self-care journey so you can know me a little better.

From an early age, I've been fascinated by people, the way we interact, the way we think and the reasons we do the things we do.

This curiosity and drive for knowledge to understand me, and to support others to gain a deep understanding of their personal experience, has led to me studying both personal & professional development. As well as working jobs in the helping and holistic therapy spaces offering body and talking therapies.

But even with all this knowledge, I had disconnected from what I needed.

When I didn't look after myself, my life wasn't in my best interest. I was unhappy but didn't know I was unhappy. I lost touch with my boundaries and tolerated behaviours that caused harm to me.

I had stopped listening to my own inner voice, it had been discredited and discounted by people around me and I no longer trusted my own knowing.

I was doing what society told me I should be doing to be happy, so I should have been happy, right?

No, I wasn't...I was living in a complete stress state and not completely aware of it because it had just become my normal state.

I didn't look after myself on a soul level. Superficially yes, but in a way that really filled me up and made me know that I was living my life the best way for me, that I wasn't doing.

For me, my self-care journey as it is now really started by leaving an unhealthy long-term relationship and the business I had created with a friend, but that is a story for another day.

Once I was in a space of more calm, I started to experience physical issues that led me to be diagnosed with a chronic health condition. It was almost as if my body knew it was now safe to breathe and was telling me it needed space to heal. At this point, I had, of course, been in the habit of ignoring my own needs and my body as it gently whispered to me. I hadn't listened to my own body for so long that it decided it was time to shout…and shout it did!

I went from working as a holistic therapist, running my own salon space, and spending my days doing therapeutic massages & coaching sessions to help others feel well, to finding myself in the position of being practically bed-ridden and needing to really pay attention to my own needs.

I was in constant pain, fatigued, experiencing brain fog, forgetfulness, muscle weakness and various other random symptoms.

I was diagnosed with chronic health conditions and told this was life now…... I wasn't ok with accepting that and realised it was time to really focus on applying all the information I had been giving to my clients to support their wellness and start to dive deeper into my own self-care journey.

Along the way, I learnt about meditation, practised mindfulness, and started to connect deeper by listening to how my own body and intuition spoke to me.

I spent time healing my trauma, calming my nervous system, and unpicking the unhelpful messages I had picked up about myself along the way.

I learnt to trust & choose my own voice again, became more connected to my own needs and understood that putting myself first, practicing radical self-care and nourishing myself allowed me to have a healthier, happier relationship with myself & others.

By choosing to nourish me I now live in a state of peace & contentment, I find gratitude in the everyday moments and surround myself with people who also wish to do the same.

I had been on my own journey for a decade before I started my podcast *Conversations with Sarah*, created The SRTT Self-Care Club membership and decided to write this book.

My hope with this book is that it is easy to digest and that it will inspire you to know that you can create space to nourish yourself and that you will also start your self-care journey.

So back to the question…who am I?

Today, as I write this,

I am

Mum

Wife

Sister

Aunt

Friend

The Self-Care Queen

Reformed people pleaser

Chronic health warrior

Connector of people

Purple leopard print leggings wearer

Asker of questions

Dancer of my own beat

Sponge of knowledge

Seer of solutions

Creator

Facilitator

Tutor

Selectively social ambivert

Ever growing

On my mission to educate, empower and enable women to prioritise themselves and create a life they love with healthy habits & a success mindset.

Passionate about supporting other women to feel not only able, but also worthy of creating space to look after their own needs.

Driven to use my own formal learning and life experiences to create and share tools to support others in making change possible.

Host of a weekly wellness podcasts

Spiritual explorer

Dreamer

Healer

Soul-seeker

Ever-growing

Ever-changing

Playfully

    experiencing

        this life.

REFLECTION QUESTION

What do I currently do that I think of as Self-Care?

What is Self-Care?

Self-care is about regular daily practices that you undertake to look after yourself on all levels: physical, mental, emotional, and spiritual, so you are living in your truth and creating a life that you want.

Being able to connect with and communicate your needs to live a life that honours YOU at the core of all you do.

Yes, it is about bubble baths, skincare, dentist appointments, eating nutritious food,

BUT
it is also about knowing your boundaries, being able to love who you are, having fun, enjoying living in the moment and planning for the future you want.

Creating a self-care practice that works for you can take some unlearning, and reframing of all the things you have been told you should be doing. Through this book, we are going to explore ways to create foundational self-care practices to support you at the start of your self-care journey.

There are many elements to self-care that help create positive physical, mental & emotional health and it's important to create habits that give you a balance.

A brief overview of types of self-care for you to consider are:

Physical: The way you nurture your physical body. Physical self-care includes practices that support sleep, movement, food, rest, medical check-ups & hygiene.

Mental: Caring for your mind, allowing it the opportunity to learn new things, having moments of quiet & peace without worry and being kind in your thoughts about yourself.

Emotional: Connecting with and allowing your feelings to be. Identifying and expressing emotions, having compassion for self and others.

Spiritual: Exploring meaning and connection to others, having time alone to reflect.

Financial: Creating healthy habits with money management. Having financial security and being able to provide for your needs.

Environmental: Being in spaces that support your wellness, having a home that feels safe & welcoming.

Social: Healthy relationships with friends & family. Being part of a healthy support network and feeling a sense of belonging.

Professional: A job that feels secure and fulfilling and that provides a healthy work/life balance.

REFLECTION QUESTION

What barriers do I have to creating self-care practices?

Barriers to self-care

When we are not in the habit of looking after ourselves it is easy to become focused on all the reasons we can't possibly make space to look after our own needs. Some of the common reasons given for not being able to create regular self-care practices are:

Too busy

Fear

Feeling overwhelmed

Conditioning messages

Time

Guilt

Not knowing what to do

Is your barrier on the list?

Let's explore these reasons and start to consider how we may overcome these blocks to self-care.

Too busy

In the past there have been so many times I found myself feeling that I just didn't have time to look after myself, that I had too many other things or people that needed to be prioritised above my own needs.

It may be that you genuinely do have a busy scheduled life with commitments that you just aren't able to put down right now, that there are people that rely on you to be there and do things for them.

There may be important tasks that just won't get done if you don't do them and even when you have finished managing these tasks and expectations it feels impossible to imagine creating any time for yourself.
BUT you are here, right now, reading this book, so somewhere, somehow you have not only

recognised just how important it is to create that space for yourself, but you have also managed to do it!

So, take a moment and congratulate yourself for being here right now in this moment creating space for you and your self-care!

You are already on your journey; you are taking the steps to create space, and as you do this you will see just how powerful making time for you is, and this shift will in turn help you find opportunity to create more space.

So, I wonder, are you too busy doing things you need and want to do?

OR are you actually busy doing things you don't want to do, things you do just because you have always done them and don't know how to stop? Are you doing things that other people have asked you to do because you have no idea how to say no?

Is it possible you have fallen into the trap of pleasing everyone else and now don't know how to be less busy?

REFLECTION QUESTION

If I could say no, what would I stop doing?

Fear

When we start to connect with our own needs this can feel like an uncomfortable place to be, especially if up until now you have squished yourself and your feelings down.

For some, it can feel like you don't know where to start with it all. Feeling your emotions, hearing your thoughts, and experiencing what is happening in your life can feel like too much. Especially if you have been conditioned to not feel or express your emotions, to not talk about your needs, to not put yourself first.

It may be that you have no idea how to start doing these things and have squished down so much stuff that stopping all the busyness in your life and creating space to just be in a moment feels scary, because until now you've not allowed yourself to just be in a moment.

Up until now keeping those thoughts and feelings bottled up may have been exactly what you needed to do to be safe but it's very likely that now the things you have been keeping bottled up are starting to bubble up and are being experienced and expressed in a way that doesn't work for you.

It may be that there will be times along your self-care journey when you want to consider collaborating with a healer, therapist, coach, or holistic practitioner to support you to process and express these things in a safe way.

Perhaps you are afraid that by changing you will lose people around you, and that is a possibility. However, I would be curious about why people would prefer for you to be unhappy and live a life that isn't aligned with you.

Who is the most important person to be happy in your life?

Are YOU not the most important person to prioritise you?

Isn't the most important person to be happy with you, and the way you live your life, you?

Being able to be you and choosing yourself is one of the most important things in living a life that fills you up.

I don't mean in a way that you intentionally cause harm to others, of course, you are still going to be mindful of how you treat other people, but neglecting your own happiness shouldn't be required.

Doesn't neglecting your own happiness make it harder to be happy for others?

REFLECTION QUESTION

What am I afraid would happen if I choose my own happiness?

Feeling Overwhelmed

When we think about starting something new it's easy to feel overwhelmed by all the options that are available.

When possibilities are infinite how do we choose where to start?

Or maybe you have fallen into the trap of "all or nothing" thinking and find yourself thinking things like:

I have too much housework to do and nothing will get done if I take time for myself.

I need to spend at least an hour in the gym every day, otherwise what is the point?

I would have to give up all my favourite foods to eat more fruit & veg.

The idea of change can be overwhelming, trying new things means stepping out of your comfort zone, it means trying something that feels uncomfortable and stepping into the unknown.

All of which can feel unsafe and a little too much when you can't be sure that you won't fail.

But nothing is lost in trying something new, you don't need to be perfect at it, it's new…why would you be an expert at something you have not tried before?

At the end of this book, I have shared some suggestions to support you in creating moments of self-care. I also share tools and ideas in my membership and free groups, and a quick search on the internet will bring you more ideas than you will ever need. Once you start to create space for self-care you can play and have fun trying whatever sounds good to you.

REMEMBER if a particular self-care practice sounds like your worst nightmare, then you don't have to do it.

This is your self-care journey, you are on a different path right now, and it's ok to choose to do what feels nourishing for you.

If you have no idea what doing a particular self-care activity feels like for you then I invite you to approach the practices with an open mind, to be curious about how you may experience it, to be interested in what the experience may be like for you and allow there to be a possibility that it will nourish you and fill your cup up.

The most important thing is to start, right now, where you are, with what you have.

Think about life exactly as it is and consider how you could start to create self-care practices in what you already do.

REFLECTION QUESTION

What things do I enjoy that I have stopped doing?

Conditioning messages

As we grow, we are given messages from our family, teachers, society, and friends about how we 'should' behave, we have experiences that lead to us holding beliefs about ourselves. We may not be aware of these beliefs and will act unconsciously because of them.

Perhaps you were taught that 'nice girls' share or maybe you were praised for being quiet and putting others before yourself.

Perhaps you lived in a home with angry parents and learnt to be a peacemaker or to people-please to avoid having anger directed at you.

Maybe you were told that expressing an opinion was 'answering back' and 'disrespectful' and now you find it difficult to express your needs for fear of upsetting others.

If you grew up in a household where love and communication were withheld if you did not comply with the behaviours that were expected from you, you may find you now make unconscious choices to do things that lead to external validation for what you do for other people rather than choosing to do what you want to do.

If you were rarely given the opportunity to make your own decisions, or had your choices regularly questioned you may feel unsure in your decision-making or describe yourself as indecisive.

The good news is that you can become more aware of how you act unconsciously, and become aware of your triggers, and reactions. You can then create opportunities to make conscious choices and create change.

REFLECTION QUESTION

If I didn't consider what other people thought about me, what would I do differently?

Time

When we think of self-care we may be thinking about big things we need to create lots of time for, and if you are able to schedule those things into your daily/weekly commitments to yourself that is amazing and I am sincerely so happy that you are at a place on your self-care journey where you are able to not only realise the importance of investing time in you, but also able to consistently create that time to invest your energy into yourself.

But for many of us starting our self-care journey, we know the importance of making the commitment to ourselves, we are ready to take that step, and are just working out how to create the space.

I am NOT going to be the person that tells you to get up at 5am and do an hour of yoga &

meditation before everyone else wakes up in the morning – If that is what interests you then YES do it! If you are an early bird who feels most nourished by waking up before everyone else and taking that time to move your body and centre yourself then again YES, do it.

If this is what you want to do, make that commitment to yourself, set the alarm a little earlier, organise your clothes the night before so they are ready to go, and get up in the morning and be thankful that you have the opportunity to spend the time checking in with yourself, moving your body and starting the morning in the way that fills your cup.

But you don't have to do that if that isn't what appeals to you!

For you, creating space for yourself may need to start with smaller moments.

It may be that you need to let go of some of the expectations you are placing on yourself, expectations to always be busy, to be productive.

You may need to consider delegating some of the household tasks you do if you live with others, or give yourself permission to reduce, or stop, doing tasks you don't actually enjoy and don't need to do.

Maybe you could spend less time watching TV you aren't interested in, or perhaps there is time on your lunch break to take a moment to do something that will bring you calm. If you find yourself doom scrolling, absorbing negative news and observing toxic people on social media, that is just could you instead replace that with a habit that brings you joy?

Being aware of how you spend your time can help you to consider what conscious choices you want to make to create more time for what you want to do in your life.

REFLECTION QUESTION

If I had time, what would I want to do?

Guilt

Maybe the idea of taking time just for you fills you with guilt, the idea of creating space for you to do things, **just for you** feels like you are being selfish, or that by choosing to put yourself first you are letting other people down.

You find yourself thinking of the things you need to do for others before you will take time for yourself, or maybe you think that you should be doing things like tidy your home or do your work before you feel ok to rest, or do something that is just for the fun of doing it.

But what if you doing things for yourself meant you would have more energy and more compassion for the people around you?

Would you still feel selfish then?

REFLECTION QUESTION

What can I give myself permission to do just for me?

Not Knowing what do

There are so many things we are told that we should be doing, different expectations of what should be fun for adults and how we should be being productive. What if all those things we think we should be doing is exactly what is stopping us finding the things we love to do?

If you have been reading from start to finish and doing the reflections and exercises you have already experienced self-care practices and you are creating a growth mindset by reflecting on your current habits and that is all part of self-care.

WOOHOO! Yay you!

    You are doing it

I'm sending you a high five!

So now it's time to be more curious about the things you would like to be doing, and it may be that as soon as you take a moment to consider what you would like to do with your time, all those reasons you can't do them start to pop up. Maybe you'll just discount things because they cost too much money, feel too hard, need too much organising, won't be fun to do on your own and think about every reason to not allow yourself to make you a priority.

So, let's just for this moment, pretend that none of those things exist. Take a moment to let your imagination run wild with possibility, no matter how unrealistic, expensive, or unattainable it may feel right now. Let your imagination have fun thinking about all the things you could do if you had the time, money, and energy and no one telling you that you can't.

REFLECTION QUESTION

If there were no barriers, what new things would I like to try?

Self-care is an act of love

At its core, self-care is an act of self-love, and means choosing ourselves, even when it may mean others are upset with our choices.

Self-love means holding a healthy, loving relationship with yourself, loving yourself as you are in this moment and wanting to make an investment in your own health, personal growth, and happiness.

Being kind to yourself, giving yourself permission to do the things to look after your physical, mental & emotional health.

Giving yourself space to do things that bring you joy and happiness, as well as finding joy in the day-to-day mundane tasks that we need to perform.

When we can allow ourselves to feel and act lovingly towards ourselves something magical starts to happen, and not only do we treat ourselves better, but we also stop allowing others to treat us poorly.

What would you do if your best friend said that they were never allowed to do things just for themselves, that they were forbidden to do things just for the joy of doing them and that not only did everything they do have to bring happiness to other people but that they had no worth as a person unless they were doing things to make other people happy?

I imagine you would feel quite strongly about that, perhaps you would feel angry that someone was telling them those things, perhaps you would feel sad that they were believing what they were being told.

Would you be saying something different to your friend? Or do you agree with the statement that we are only of value if we are ignoring our own wants, and needs and doing things to make people happy?

I am going to guess that you would be encouraging your friend to stop listening to the person who is saying that to them and suggesting to them that they are an amazing person who absolutely deserves to have a life in which they feel safe, content and loved.

There is no doubt that they are not only allowed to do things for themselves but that they absolutely need to start taking steps to do things that they enjoy doing, and that give them a sense of worth and fulfilment.

You would want your friend to stop listening to that voice and to treat themselves with loving kindness,
wouldn't you?

YES?

So, why wouldn't you demand that for yourself?

REFLECTION QUESTION

What do you currently do to treat yourself with loving kindness?

How do you talk to yourself?

One of the ways we can be more loving towards ourselves is in the way we self-talk.

The person you spend the most time with and who has the most impact on your mindset is YOU!

So, what is self-talk?

Self-talk, or our inner voice is the way our brain communicates our conscious & unconscious beliefs. It is a combination of "truths" we have accepted based on how we have interpreted our experiences, and messages we have accepted from others, things people have said to us and things we have interpreted from another person's words, action, or tone.

Our self-talk is also influenced by societal, religious, cultural and gender expectations.

The way we speak to and about ourselves holds power, it can influence the way we feel about ourselves and how we experience life.

The way in which you talk to yourself in your mind and out loud impacts the way in which you see yourself and the things you will believe you are able to do.

Notice your self-talk: Are you using kind and encouraging words?

Do you motivate & celebrate yourself or are you critical & judgemental?

Your self-talk does not always tell the truth, especially when you are stressed, tired, having a challenging time or if something didn't go according to plan, thinking can spiral down and lead you to get caught in a trap of negative self-talk.

Negative self-talk can impact your physical, emotional and mental health. Being critical and unkind to yourself generally leads to feelings of unhappiness, reducing confidence and being demotivated. It can prevent you from trying new experiences and make you believe that you are not good enough. It can also have a physical effect on your body and may be experienced as pain and fatigue.

Once you realise that your self-talk is negative you can take steps to change the way you think and learn to treat yourself with loving kindness. Allowing your inner critic to talk to yourself with unkindness is not being loving towards yourself. If you do not love who you are, self-care can seem impossible.

Learning to like and love yourself, or at least be able to love yourself, even if you do not always like yourself, is essential to creating a life where you make choices to support your best interests.

A place to start creating love towards yourself is in the way you speak to yourself.

The first step to making a change to self-talk is to notice the way you talk to yourself.

Our brains are wired to naturally notice negatives; however, we can change that by being more consciously aware of the positive and the same goes for self-talk!
Often our mind is exaggerating a negative and is not only being unkind but also untrue. Aloud

it can be a way to laugh off insecurity or bring up a worry before someone else does.... but remember your words have power and you have the power to choose your words!

Creating a more positive self-talk can start by learning to catch the critic.... when you notice you are being unkind to yourself (either in your own mind or speaking aloud) hit the pause button...and ask yourself....

Is this thought true?

Is this thought kind?

Would I say this to a friend?

Using Positive affirmations can help you to challenge the subconscious mind, quiet the critic and change your self-talk. Repeating short positive statements to encourage a more positive mindset and be more loving towards yourself can be a powerful tool especially if you are able to create statements that feel aligned.

For some of us, saying affirmations can feel frustrating or like lying to ourselves if the statements are too far removed from how we currently feel about ourselves.

I encourage you to consider affirmations like a coat. It is something you can try on, see how it feels and tailor to adapt it to be a better fit for you in the now, if you want to.

If you say an affirmation but find yourself having an uncomfortable reaction to what you are saying I suggest being curious about the reaction you are having to the affirmation. Notice how you feel about what you are saying and explore what's going on underneath for you.

For example, if you are saying I feel confident and that feels wrong, explore what is going on for you and what feels ok, perhaps you need to adapt it to
'I feel confident when….. and adding something you do feel confident doing, and embracing that feeling, embracing that confidence, and then stepping into that confidence in other parts of your life.

Practising self-compassion also helps to reduce stress and anxiety, it encourages you to let go of judgments that you place on yourself and others.

Letting go of perfection and allowing yourself to make mistakes without criticism supports you in building a loving relationship with yourself.

So, if you are honest, could you be a little kinder to yourself?

I think for many of us the answer is yes!

ACTIVITY

This is my invitation to you to celebrate yourself today! I'd love for you to take some time to give yourself a heartfelt compliment, say something that you would say to a friend.

Maybe it will be hard to do, or perhaps even impossible, and that's ok.
This is all an opportunity to be mindful of your self-talk and practice self-compassion.

If you have already started to be critical of yourself, take a moment to pause, notice those thoughts as they pop up but try not to grab hold of them.

You don't need to push the words down or try to squish the feelings away either, you are aiming to be mindful of your thoughts, that means to just notice them, much like we would notice a cloud in the sky, without attaching meaning to it, just being aware that the thought exists, and being open to consider that although it exists it does not mean it is true.

Look yourself in the eye in a mirror and give yourself a heart-felt compliment.

Suggestions for compliments:

I am kind

I have chosen a beautiful outfit today

I am a loving person

I am brave

I am creative

I have an amazing sense of humour

I am beautiful just as I am

I am honest

I give the best hugs

ACTIVITY REFLECTIONS

First, congratulate yourself for trying, and remember it's ok if you didn't do exactly what you thought you should be doing. I encourage you to take a few moments to reflect on the activity, you can free-write whatever comes to mind or perhaps ask yourself these questions.

- How easy was it to think of, or pick a compliment?
- How did it feel to look myself in the eye?
- How did it feel to speak a compliment to myself?
- Was it easier or harder than I expected?
- Noticing the untruths of the inner critic - What negative things did I notice myself think/say?

Page for reflections

Page for reflections

Creating more positive Self-Talk

Now that you are more aware of your self-talk and how it feels to offer yourself self-compassion you can be aware if this is a place you may wish to commit to start to make changes.

Using your list from the reflection in the last activity: What untruths does your inner critic want you to believe?

Start to consider ways to reframe the negatives into a more compassionate or positive statement

Instead of these untruths	Reframe examples: Try
I am stupid	I don't know everything and that's ok.
I always make bad choices	I am learning to make choices that are in my best interest

My Untruths   My Reframes

Self-Care Practice Activities

Have you noticed that you have already started to create self-care practices?

By taking time to answer these reflection questions you are connecting into your inner world, your thoughts & feelings, your wants and your needs.

You are already being mindful and have taken the time to notice your self-talk.

You have started to be more aware of being compassionate towards yourself and are working to create a more positive mindset by giving yourself compliments and using affirmations.

I encourage you to take some time and celebrate yourself for exploring these practices and if that inner critic is popping up to remind you that you missed any sections in the book tell them THAT'S OK! You have chosen to do the task in the way that worked for you at the time you were doing them

You can choose to go back to any part of the book and do it for the first time or repeat it at any time you wish!

Remember, this is your journey, and you get to choose how you navigate it!

Making the commitment to yourself to take just 5 minutes to pause and reset can make such a difference.

I invite you to think about ways you can "take 5", that is, to play with committing to taking 5 minutes in each day to do something just for you.

In the following pages I am sharing some "take 5" ideas for you to consider and try out.

These are easy, actionable activities that you probably already have included in your day-to-day routine that you can just tweak to create a more mindful approach, so that they become more nourishing self-care practices.

Shower

Make having a shower a mindful experience, approach the activity as

'I get to take time for myself'

rather than

'I must make time to wash'.

Leave your phone in another room, bring a clean, fluffy comfortable towel into the bathroom, and pick your favourite products to wash with.

Take in some deep breaths before you even get into the shower and when you step into it and feel the water, bring your awareness to how the water feels on your body, how the temperature & the pressure feels.

If you notice your mind wandering to things that have happened in the day or things you need to do next – bring your attention back to the water, the way it sounds as it falls from the shower head, how the droplets feel as they touch your skin.

Pay attention to the smell of the bubbles as you wash and the pressure on your skin as you wash yourself.

When you turn off the water again take a moment to focus on your natural breath as you step out of the shower and wrap yourself in your towel.

Notice the aroma of the clean towel and how the texture feels as you take time to dry yourself, perhaps you'll notice how relaxed your muscles feel, as you take time to lovingly apply skin care products to your face and body you'll notice how the texture of your skin feels and changes as it absorbs the products you use.

Any time your mind wanders you don't need to be critical of yourself just gently bring your attention back to the now, the sounds, scents, temperature, textures, and pressure you are experiencing.

Morning Drink

Rather than rushing to make your drink in the morning and drinking it as you rush around doing other tasks perhaps you may consider creating a relaxing self-care practice out of the daily task.

Maybe you choose a special mug to drink from, maybe you currently drink on the go as you drive and instead will pop it in a flask and take a moment to pay attention as you drink it in the car before you start work.

When you make your drink, give it your full attention: pay attention to the sound of the water as you fill the kettle, notice the kettle as it boils, the change in the sounds it makes, the steam as it wafts out the spout, the way the water changes as it meets your tea bag or coffee or powdered drink, pay attention as you stir your drink, do you notice yourself feel the need to rush or can you be deliberate in the circles you make as you stir.

Notice the temperature of your cup in your hand, the smell of your drink as the aroma reaches your nose before you even take a sip and taste it. With every sip take a moment to really feel the liquid in your mouth, bring awareness to how the temperature feels, what the taste is like for you and the sensation as you swallow. Take a moment to breathe and savour each mouthful before you move onto the next.

Any time you notice your mind wandering, be kind to yourself and gently bring your attention back to the now and the way the cup feels in your hand, the smell, temperature and taste you are experiencing.

Breathing

You already breathe, all day every day without thinking about it.

Making a regular, conscious decision to bring your attention to your breath and using deep breathing exercises can help reduce stress, and anxiety, reduce pain and has a whole host of other positive benefits.

You may wish to do this practice on the hour every hour, or perhaps you'll choose to do it as you move from activity to activity throughout the day or find another way that works for you.

You may find another breathing exercise that you enjoy but I invite you to take 3 deep breaths. You may find it useful to count to 4 with each breath in and out.

1. You can be standing, seated, or even laying down, place one hand on your chest and the other on your abdomen, letting your neck & shoulders relax

2. Breathe in slowly and deeply through your nose, feeling the hand on your stomach rise…hold the breath for a count of 4

3. Slowly breathe out through your mouth feeling the stomach deflate. Holding for a count of 4 and then repeating from step 1.

You will most probably find that even this short, focused breathing exercise, leaves you feeling more relaxed and centred as you move through your day.

Dancing

Dancing is an amazing form of self-expression, it is a quick and easy way to shift your energy as well as having all the physical benefits we get from movement.

If you immediately discount dancing, I invite you to spend some time connecting to what is going on for you that you can't consider spending time moving to music.

Perhaps it is because you feel like you can't do it well or feel self-conscious, but this isn't a show, or a competition. This is a self-expression, this is about connecting with your feelings, expressing them, and if needed releasing them.

There is no wrong way of doing it.

As with any physical activity, gently ease your body into movement by using stretches before and after dancing. Always listen to your body, don't ignore any pain and niggles, and remember to stay hydrated.

When you are ready to move, put on some music and gently stretch and move your body to warm the muscles and move to the music however your body wants to, move in whatever way feels right to you in the moment. This is not about thinking, or creating a perfect dance routine, this is about connecting into your emotions with the music, by feeling the beat, the words, the rhythm. Start by swaying your hips or waving your arms and see where the feelings take you.

Dance to your own beat and allow your emotions to be expressed with your movement however you wish.

The power of meditation

When I first tried meditation, it felt such an uncomfortable thing to do. In my mind I had the image of a person sitting with crossed legs on top of a mountain, chanting. I imagined that they had a completely clear and calm mind and were able to sit still and be completely in the moment. As someone who's always fidgeting in one way or another with at least 14 tabs open in my brain, it seemed that it would be impossible to sit still and empty my mind. Listening to guided meditations was also a struggle, I would find the person's voice annoying, or the pace just didn't feel right for me – I placed a pressure on myself to be what I imagined someone who meditated was and I couldn't be that.

I understood that meditation was an amazing tool for relaxation and to reset the nervous system but couldn't picture how I practised in a way that worked for me. So, as with many things I wanted to understand, I took a training course in how to teach meditation. I started to learn about the several types of meditation and realised that there were times within my life I naturally fell into a state of mindfulness, and that opened my mind to the possibility that I could also meditate. As with many things I do I needed to make the practice work for me, so if like me you think you are someone who can't meditate, I invite you to let go of the idea you have of what meditating is and play with what can work for you. You may also discover that you naturally find yourself in a state of meditation in your day-to-day activities.

So let's start by doing an exploration of what comes to mind when you think about meditation. Do you imagine something similar to my previous ideas? Or do you picture something completely different? Do you have any previous experience with meditation? What was good and what wasn't great about that experience?

Maybe it is something you already do and have started to feel the benefits from and are reading this chapter because you are curious what my thoughts are about it. If that's the case – maybe now is a good time to take a moment and imagine what the perfect meditation for you may be.

As you read this, how do you picture yourself being when you try meditation…. Where are you…. are you in a hall with other people, are you outside in nature, are you at home….?

Perhaps you are positioned exactly as you are right now in this moment…is it comfortable or do you want to move to a different position.

Perhaps you imagine that you are seated on the floor…or in a chair…. maybe you are laying down on the sofa, bed, in the bath or on a yoga mat on the floor. … Do you have a blanket…or a pillow…. How does your body feel right now, in this perfect for you meditation practice?

How do you breathe?

Do you breathe in and out through your mouth or are you able to draw the breath in through your nose and pull it all the way down into your stomach and sigh it out through your mouth….do you notice the rise and fall of your stomach as the breath moves in and out of your body?

Are you able to notice the temperature of the breath as you breathe in and out…perhaps it feels a little cool…. or maybe it's a little warm…. however it is, it is just right for you in this moment……..

And as you are focused on the breath coming in and out of your body you may notice that thoughts jump into your mind, knocking on your brain asking to be listened to…and that's ok if they do…you can notice them….you can acknowledge they exist….you can also let them fade away for now…. perhaps they float into your mind…like little bubbles floating into your awareness…. or like a cloud you are watching float across the sky….

How does your body feel? Are you feeling tense or relaxed? Do you need to move and shift yourself into a more comfortable position? …..as you breathe in and out do you notice how your body shifts and changes as your muscles start to gently relax, as they let go of any stress or strain they are holding onto…..and perhaps you may find that you are breathing just a little deeper ……..and with each breath maybe you notice you are becoming more and more relaxed….. as you start to just be right here in this moment of meditation.

What next?

Firstly, let's take a moment to celebrate that you have made it to what's next. By reading this book you have started to create space to nourish you and are ready to take the next steps on your self-care journey.

Maybe you may wish to revisit some of the reflection questions and notice if there are some answers you have given yourself for what you are now ready to put into action.

You have the 'Take 5' activities that you may wish to make a regular part of your daily routine and you may also start to notice other places in your life you can take moments to be mindful and allow yourself space to pause.

I, of course, would love to connect with you and support you on the next stage of your self-care journey.

Do you use social media?

Yes? Then you can find me at @srttselfcare on most social media platforms, if you pop it into a search engine I should pop up. I spend most of my social media time on Facebook and that is where I host my free group that you'd be most welcome to join. In the group we have daily prompt posts, and all are encouraged to ask questions, celebrate wins, ask for support and share what they wish along their self-care journey. As well as lots of free information in the guides to support you with your next steps.

You can listen to Conversations with Sarah Podcast, where guests join me with stories of hope and healing and where wellness practitioners share different ways to support your self-care. You'll find the link to my group and other free resources such as the E-magazine and my podcast on my website www.srtt.co.uk

If you are ready to take the step to create change and invest in yourself, you may wish to join my online membership. In The SRTT Self-Care Club, you have access to guided meditations, mindset & motivation videos, hypnotherapy, workshops, distance energy healing and our beautiful supportive community.

Whatever you choose to do next, I hope that you continue to make the choice to nourish you!

Sarah

Printed in Great Britain
by Amazon